Pouring from the cup of my mind

Crystal Nielsen

BookLeaf Publishing
India | USA | UK

Presentation by *BookLeaf Publishing*

Web: www.bookleafpub.com

E-mail: info@bookleafpub.com

ISBN : 9789357447430

First edition 2021

DEDICATION

Thank you to those I've shared my journey with of all lengths of every outcome.

Welcome

I hold my fiercest emotions to myself.
For no one truly loves me for all I am now,
In this moment, after my rollercoaster of time
I share but I also hide i had any part in it
Im fearful to be vulnerable
To be soft or gentle
For its in those moments i can be torn to pieces

Rollercoaster

My mind is is an everchanging theme park
A turbulent rollercoaster
Full of screams and smiles as it twists and
climbs
A warm memory
A sadness at an end
A chalm chaos about to errupt that i still cant
master

Is this growth

Repeated past patterns
Heightened self awareness
This is thw first leap in your peronal growth
You are not going backwards
You are taking note of your past
Accept that sometime you need to repeat the
pattern to know it it not your path
Take note, be aware
This is still progress

After

The room is empty
but it still echoes of past laughter
A song still brings you to the front of our minds
I sit in silence tonight but i still talk to you
It happens from time to time
A family so broken
Full of such crippling sorrow after

Stories

You spoke to me in ways no other had
Like an entirely new lauguage i never had to
study
It was all i needed to hear
And it was almost painful to turn away,to not to
listen
I heard mountains and valleys
Oceans and forrests
It was impossible to hear anything else but your
story
But you asked me questions about stories i
shared as if id never even spoke

The helping hands

I stopped asking for help long ago
I learnt young that not everyone that is supposed
to love and nuture is capable
Ive watched those i opened up to and shared my
pians
Lie, cheat, steal my time, my love my peace
Im no longer really sure what a helping hand
looks like
When i look at mine they are filled with scars
Ive leant my hand my whole life to quench
others thirst for blood
See their fingers where shaped like teeth

Have i failed

My life i thought id be a mother
I thought of all of everything in the world i
would give
Then I felt you, i saw you and i was terrified, not
ready and neither was he.
Then I wasnt and we werent an us
The date still has me under blankets for a day
filled with what ifs
Angry, broken
I protected myself from that pain again and not
looked back but in the silence i wonder and hope
But my mind then battles itself i feel relieved
and selfish in carefree plans and time
Perhaps its not for me perhaps im scared ill hurt
a child as i was
But the what if knocks and i cant think past the
I failed already

You

You noticed things about my body
Things i now love id never even seen truly
Tho you were only ever temporary
You pushed permanent limits of what
relationships could be
You loved what you found for every second
unlike what id known before
Yet we knew it wouldnt be life so i turned away
Thank you for the connection
For it being so free, open as if you were only
mine
As if it were multiple of how long id had you
As if you werent tethered to another
People didnt understand but you cant unless it
knocks on your own door
Perhaps we saved each other in those moments
To be truly seen, felt and all forms of blissfully
naked
Thank you

The titanic

Id never loved anyone the way i loved them
Even as they didnt choose me
We gravitated back to each other as if a lifetime
had passed
He held me in my true lowest points of swlf
worth, of grief and i him in his hatred of being
stuck in this life
I felt seen in the fleeting moments where i was
more than the liquor more than the drugs that
came after that no longer covered the pain
It was truly beautiful but a titanic of pain
My heart tore to see you cry at the loss of your
brother another decade later of no contact
For your family were always mine even after it
all even after we sank

The lucky ones

It is not worse for the ones who one day realise
Its agony for the ones who never dreamt of
taking it for granted
Who saw the light and shade and chose all of it.
ALL
who gripped with two hands but could only look
on as they lost the love they loved the most
"Some people dont know what they lost until its
gone"
It ripped fast like a band aid
Those are the lucky ones

Times mistake

Time has made a mistake... surely
For i am still waiting, still hoping

A mistake

And has saved us but moment to find each other
again

Had i known

If i had known it was the last time id hear your voice id have played your favourite music and asked you to sing

Id have stared.
Stared a little longer at how you smile and the reases a life of love and laughter have left across your face

Id have held your hand longer, tighter

A minute could have laster a year
Hand i known it was the last time

Slow dancing

Not everyone is meant to stay
But my soul just knew who it was meant to slow
dance with in an empty bar to its own music
It recognised its own light
And in that blip of eternity that lasted but a
minute it was beautifully mirrored by yours

Now it replays in quiet stolen seconds as if theyd
danced in lifetimes before and like theyd never
stopped

Time

In the heat and the dark of it all its not one day at
a time
Its a hell of lot of gruelling one hour at a time
And one minute at a time in those hours feel like
years
Its not one day at a time but im working hard on
my "one" to get there

Feel

Every once in a while im left with nothing

No choice
But to feel

All i have pushed away, tried to forget, lost and
found
And it rushes over me in waves
And i sink

Go figure

I hurt with a pain far deeper than physical
Im hollow like your words
I sit and question everything
'Til all space and time are blurred

I choose the ache that feels familiar
Is this the path from here?
Thats the silent killer
A wicked twisted circle .... go figure

Nannan

Papa's here with us now i promise to drive him a
little mad
I promise not to grieve forever, i know itd make
you sad
I can hear the "stop making a fuss", shed hope
we carry on
I know no doubt, youll sit by me when i listen to
your songs
I promise i wont feel guilt in laughter & we will
always know how much you care
I wont regret a smile that you wknt be here to
share
I promise to talk about the good times in a hope
a word i might say
Will help someone recapture a memory with you
For a minute... an hour... or a day

Swim

Ive sat by and watched as i poured from my
reserve into others they move on happily
Ive then gasped for air as if drowning and
watched no one dove in
But its those who i never thought id even been a
blip to that share ..
that I mean something to them and they
genuinely care
Those are the people i resonate with

I have no breath for those scared to face whats
real
Scared to dive and swim with me when im in the
deep end

Stranger

Its sad to think you never tried for years of my
life
Then you waltz back in with stories of your wife
A man thats never been my father but says hes a
Dad
all youve said is your side and you havnt asked
about me a tad?
You soeak about a bond we shared as if id even
know
Your a complete stranger to me i have no
memories to show
I hope you find youre peace you need if you are
truly ill
That will not come from me believe me it never
will

www.ingramcontent.com/pod-product-compliance
Lightning Source LLC
Chambersburg PA
CBHW050753180726
48003CB00020B/2558